Fire, Fire
Burning Bright

For Alexandra and Harry—J.B.
For Evelyne Johnson—H.P.

Produced by Daniel Weiss Associates, Inc.
33 West 17 Street, New York, NY 10011

Text copyright © 1990 Daniel Weiss Associates, Inc.,
and Al Jarnow

Illustration copyright © 1990 Heidi Petach

Published by Silver Press, a division of
Silver Burdett Press, Inc., Simon & Schuster, Inc.
Prentice Hall Bldg., Englewood Cliffs, NJ 07632
For information address: Silver Press.

Printed in the United States of America
10 9 8 7 6 5 4 3 2 1

Library of Congress Cataloging-in-Publication Data

Barkan, Joanne.
Fire, fire burning bright / by Joanne Barkan; illustrated
by Heidi Petach.
p.   cm.—(First facts)
Summary: A simple introduction to the origins, properties, uses,
and dangers of fire.
1. Fire—Juvenile literature.   [1. Fire.]   I. Petach, Heidi,
ill.   II. Title.   III. Series: First facts
(Englewood Cliffs, N.J.)
QD516.B28 1990   89-24146
541.3'61—dc20   CIP
*   AC*
ISBN 0-671-68658-5   ISBN 0-671-68654-2 (lib. bdg.)

First Facts™

Fire, Fire Burning Bright

Written by Joanne Barkan
Illustrated by Heidi Petach

Silver Press

In the wind, see me flutter.
Feed me more, and I will grow.
Drops of water make me sputter.
In the dark, I'm sure to glow.
What am I?

Think about the many types of fire
you see everyday.
You might see a lighted match.
Or the flames from a gas stove.
Or a dancing fire in the fireplace.

And once a year—on your special day—
the flickering candles on your birthday cake.

People have been using fire
for thousands and thousands of years.
Imagine what it was like
to live in a cave a long time ago.

You would make a fire
to keep warm and to cook food.
At night, your only light would come from fire.

Could dangerous animals sneak up on you?
Don't worry! Your fire would frighten them away.

People who lived long ago
learned to use fire in other ways, too.
They used fire to bake clay pots.
Then the pots were hard enough to
hold food and water.

With fire, they softened metal and shaped it into tools.
These metal axes, hammers, and knives helped them work faster and better.

Today we still use fire to cook food,
to keep warm, to make tools, and to bake clay.
But just think of all the new ways we use fire.

When a grown-up starts the engine of a car,
off it goes!
The engine burns gasoline.
That means it uses fire to make the car move.

spark plug

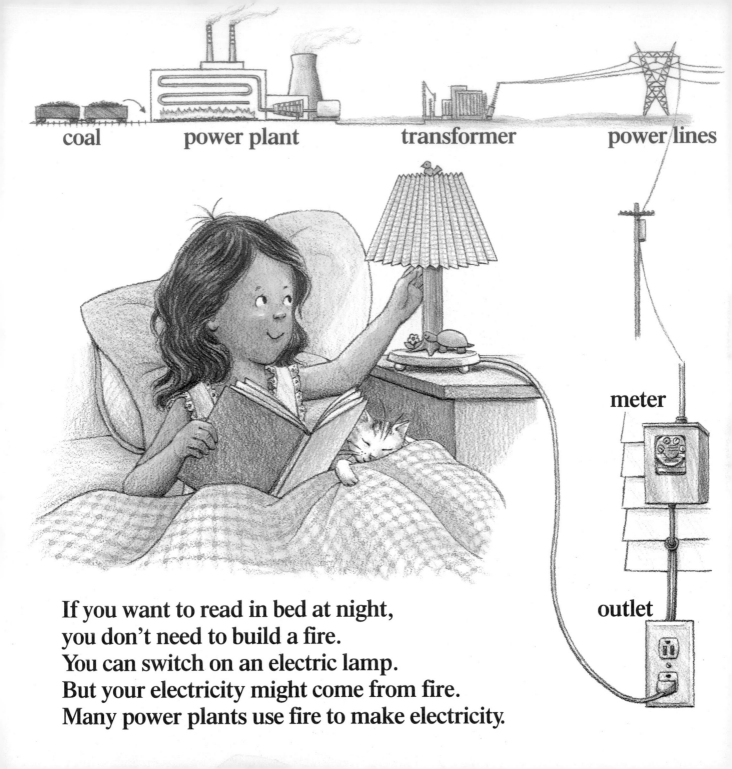

coal   power plant   transformer   power lines

meter

outlet

If you want to read in bed at night,
you don't need to build a fire.
You can switch on an electric lamp.
But your electricity might come from fire.
Many power plants use fire to make electricity.

Without fire, factories couldn't make steel for trains, planes, roller coasters, or ice skates.

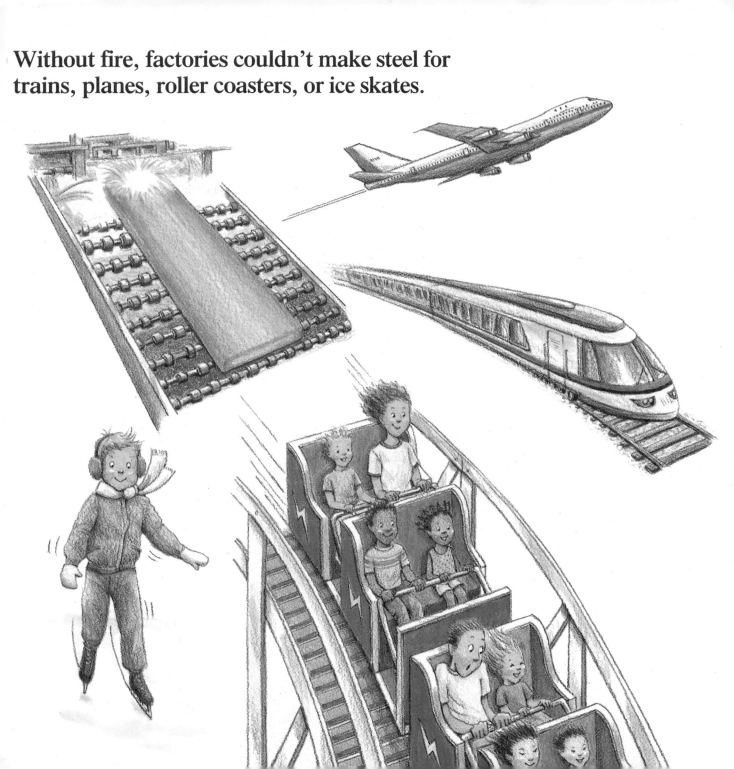

What is fire?
Ask a grown-up to light a candle in a dark room.
What do you notice about the flame?
As the candle burns, it gives off light.
Now carefully hold your hand
a few inches from the flame.
It gives off heat, too, doesn't it?
Fire is both the light and heat that are made
when something is burning.

There can be no fire
unless there is something to burn.
Whatever burns is called fuel.
The wax and string wick of your candle are fuel.
What about the fire in a fireplace?
The wood logs are fuel.

And the gas piped into your stove is the fuel that cooks your blueberry pancakes.

Not all fuels burn in the same way.
The flames from a gas stove are bright blue.

The flame of a lighted match is yellow and blue.

What about charcoal burning in a barbecue grill?
There's no flame at all! The charcoal glows red.

Some fuels make smoke when they burn.
Smoke contains tiny particles of fuel
that haven't burned completely.
Blow out a candle.
As soon as the flame goes out,
smoke will rise from the wick.

Every fire needs oxygen to burn.
You can't see oxygen—
it's an invisible gas in the air
all around you.

Have a grown-up put an upside-down glass
over a lighted candle.
Watch the flame get weaker and weaker.
Then—pouf!—out it goes.
The flame can't burn after it uses up
all the oxygen in the glass.

We need fire, but it can be very dangerous.
Fires can spread quickly and
burn out of control.
They can destroy houses and schools,
and burn down forests.
Fires can hurt people and animals, too.

So be careful!
Unless you are with a grown-up,
don't go near anything that's burning.

If a fire starts—quick!—
call the fire department.
Firefighters use heavy hoses
to spray water on a fire.

They rescue people who are trapped.
They pull away burning wood
so the fire will have less fuel.
They cover the fire
with chemical sprays and foams.
Then the fire can't get oxygen.

Some fuels burn so quickly that they explode. You hear a loud BOOM because the exploding fuel suddenly gives off a huge amount of gas.

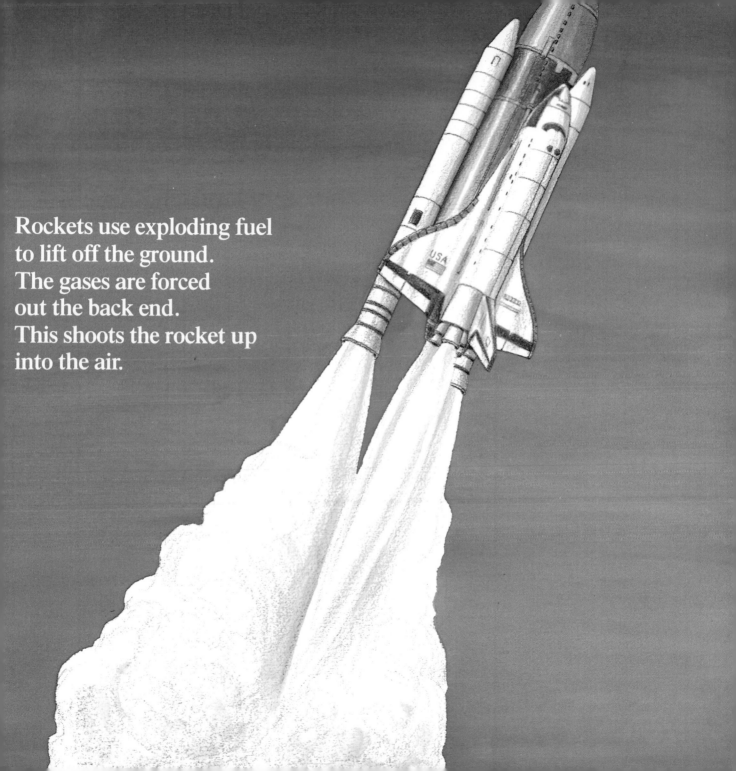

Rockets use exploding fuel
to lift off the ground.
The gases are forced
out the back end.
This shoots the rocket up
into the air.

One kind of explosion is lots of fun: fireworks!
How do fireworks work?

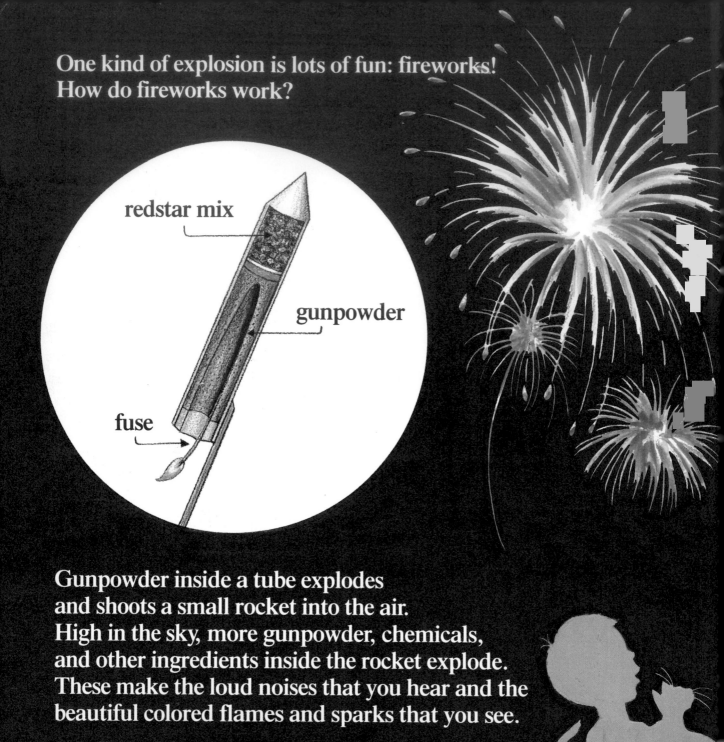

redstar mix

gunpowder

fuse

Gunpowder inside a tube explodes
and shoots a small rocket into the air.
High in the sky, more gunpowder, chemicals,
and other ingredients inside the rocket explode.
These make the loud noises that you hear and the
beautiful colored flames and sparks that you see.

Fireworks for fun.
Electricity for light.
A furnace to keep you warm.
All the fires you need are burning, burning bright!